Journal

Copyright Ponderings Australia Pty Ltd 2021
www.ponderings.com.au

PO Box 353 Leopold, VIC 3224
media@ponderings.com.au
Cover image by RawPixel creative commons
Graphic design by Jenny Watson and Kirtsten Macdonald

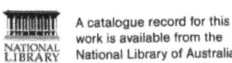 A catalogue record for this work is available from the National Library of Australia

ISBN: 978-0-6450309-0-7

DAILY PLANNER

TODAY IS A NEW DAY FULL OF POSSIBILITY

DATE

WATER INTAKE

MY TASKLIST

MY APPOINTMENTS

HEALTH NOTES

EXERCISE

NOTES TO SELF

GRATITUDE LIST

DAILY PLANNER

TODAY IS A NEW DAY FULL OF POSSIBILITY

DATE

WATER INTAKE

MY TASKLIST

MY APPOINTMENTS

HEALTH NOTES

EXERCISE

NOTES TO SELF

GRATITUDE LIST

DAILY PLANNER
TODAY IS A NEW DAY FULL OF POSSIBILITY

DATE

WATER INTAKE

MY TASKLIST

MY APPOINTMENTS

HEALTH NOTES

EXERCISE

NOTES TO SELF

GRATITUDE LIST

DAILY PLANNER
TODAY IS A NEW DAY FULL OF POSSIBILITY

DATE

WATER INTAKE

MY TASKLIST

MY APPOINTMENTS

HEALTH NOTES

EXERCISE

NOTES TO SELF

GRATITUDE LIST

DAILY PLANNER

TODAY IS A NEW DAY FULL OF POSSIBILITY

DATE   WATER INTAKE

MY TASKLIST   MY APPOINTMENTS

HEALTH NOTES   EXERCISE

NOTES TO SELF   GRATITUDE LIST

DAILY PLANNER

TODAY IS A NEW DAY FULL OF POSSIBILITY

DATE

WATER INTAKE

MY TASKLIST

MY APPOINTMENTS

HEALTH NOTES

EXERCISE

NOTES TO SELF

GRATITUDE LIST

DAILY PLANNER
TODAY IS A NEW DAY FULL OF POSSIBILITY

DATE

WATER INTAKE

MY TASKLIST

MY APPOINTMENTS

HEALTH NOTES

EXERCISE

NOTES TO SELF

GRATITUDE LIST

DAILY PLANNER
TODAY IS A NEW DAY FULL OF POSSIBILITY

DATE

WATER INTAKE

MY TASKLIST

MY APPOINTMENTS

HEALTH NOTES

EXERCISE

NOTES TO SELF

GRATITUDE LIST

DAILY PLANNER

TODAY IS A NEW DAY FULL OF POSSIBILITY

DATE WATER INTAKE

MY TASKLIST MY APPOINTMENTS

HEALTH NOTES EXERCISE

NOTES TO SELF GRATITUDE LIST

DAILY PLANNER

TODAY IS A NEW DAY FULL OF POSSIBILITY

DATE WATER INTAKE

MY TASKLIST MY APPOINTMENTS

HEALTH NOTES EXERCISE

NOTES TO SELF GRATITUDE LIST

DAILY PLANNER

TODAY IS A NEW DAY FULL OF POSSIBILITY

DATE

WATER INTAKE

MY TASKLIST

MY APPOINTMENTS

HEALTH NOTES

EXERCISE

NOTES TO SELF

GRATITUDE LIST

DAILY PLANNER
TODAY IS A NEW DAY FULL OF POSSIBILITY

DATE

WATER INTAKE

MY TASKLIST

MY APPOINTMENTS

HEALTH NOTES

EXERCISE

NOTES TO SELF

GRATITUDE LIST

DAILY PLANNER
TODAY IS A NEW DAY FULL OF POSSIBILITY

DATE

WATER INTAKE

MY TASKLIST

MY APPOINTMENTS

HEALTH NOTES

EXERCISE

NOTES TO SELF

GRATITUDE LIST

DAILY PLANNER
TODAY IS A NEW DAY FULL OF POSSIBILITY

DATE

WATER INTAKE

MY TASKLIST

MY APPOINTMENTS

HEALTH NOTES

EXERCISE

NOTES TO SELF

GRATITUDE LIST

DAILY PLANNER

TODAY IS A NEW DAY FULL OF POSSIBILITY

DATE WATER INTAKE

MY TASKLIST MY APPOINTMENTS

HEALTH NOTES EXERCISE

NOTES TO SELF GRATITUDE LIST

DAILY PLANNER

TODAY IS A NEW DAY FULL OF POSSIBILITY

DATE

WATER INTAKE

MY TASKLIST

MY APPOINTMENTS

HEALTH NOTES

EXERCISE

NOTES TO SELF

GRATITUDE LIST

DAILY PLANNER

TODAY IS A NEW DAY FULL OF POSSIBILITY

DATE

WATER INTAKE

MY TASKLIST

MY APPOINTMENTS

HEALTH NOTES

EXERCISE

NOTES TO SELF

GRATITUDE LIST

DAILY PLANNER

TODAY IS A NEW DAY FULL OF POSSIBILITY

DATE					WATER INTAKE

MY TASKLIST				MY APPOINTMENTS

HEALTH NOTES				EXERCISE

NOTES TO SELF				GRATITUDE LIST

DAILY PLANNER
TODAY IS A NEW DAY FULL OF POSSIBILITY

DATE

WATER INTAKE

MY TASKLIST

MY APPOINTMENTS

HEALTH NOTES

EXERCISE

NOTES TO SELF

GRATITUDE LIST

DAILY PLANNER

TODAY IS A NEW DAY FULL OF POSSIBILITY

DATE

WATER INTAKE

MY TASKLIST

MY APPOINTMENTS

HEALTH NOTES

EXERCISE

NOTES TO SELF

GRATITUDE LIST

DAILY PLANNER
TODAY IS A NEW DAY FULL OF POSSIBILITY

DATE

WATER INTAKE

MY TASKLIST

MY APPOINTMENTS

HEALTH NOTES

EXERCISE

NOTES TO SELF

GRATITUDE LIST

DAILY PLANNER
TODAY IS A NEW DAY FULL OF POSSIBILITY

DATE

WATER INTAKE

MY TASKLIST

MY APPOINTMENTS

HEALTH NOTES

EXERCISE

NOTES TO SELF

GRATITUDE LIST

DAILY PLANNER

TODAY IS A NEW DAY FULL OF POSSIBILITY

DATE

WATER INTAKE

MY TASKLIST

MY APPOINTMENTS

HEALTH NOTES

EXERCISE

NOTES TO SELF

GRATITUDE LIST

DAILY PLANNER
TODAY IS A NEW DAY FULL OF POSSIBILITY

DATE

WATER INTAKE

MY TASKLIST

MY APPOINTMENTS

HEALTH NOTES

EXERCISE

NOTES TO SELF

GRATITUDE LIST

DAILY PLANNER

TODAY IS A NEW DAY FULL OF POSSIBILITY

DATE

WATER INTAKE

MY TASKLIST

MY APPOINTMENTS

HEALTH NOTES

EXERCISE

NOTES TO SELF

GRATITUDE LIST

DAILY PLANNER
TODAY IS A NEW DAY FULL OF POSSIBILITY

DATE

WATER INTAKE

MY TASKLIST

MY APPOINTMENTS

HEALTH NOTES

EXERCISE

NOTES TO SELF

GRATITUDE LIST

DAILY PLANNER
TODAY IS A NEW DAY FULL OF POSSIBILITY

DATE

WATER INTAKE

MY TASKLIST

MY APPOINTMENTS

HEALTH NOTES

EXERCISE

NOTES TO SELF

GRATITUDE LIST

DAILY PLANNER
TODAY IS A NEW DAY FULL OF POSSIBILITY

DATE

WATER INTAKE

MY TASKLIST

MY APPOINTMENTS

HEALTH NOTES

EXERCISE

NOTES TO SELF

GRATITUDE LIST

DAILY PLANNER
TODAY IS A NEW DAY FULL OF POSSIBILITY

DATE

WATER INTAKE

MY TASKLIST

MY APPOINTMENTS

HEALTH NOTES

EXERCISE

NOTES TO SELF

GRATITUDE LIST

DAILY PLANNER

TODAY IS A NEW DAY FULL OF POSSIBILITY

DATE

WATER INTAKE

MY TASKLIST

MY APPOINTMENTS

HEALTH NOTES

EXERCISE

NOTES TO SELF

GRATITUDE LIST

DAILY PLANNER
TODAY IS A NEW DAY FULL OF POSSIBILITY

DATE

WATER INTAKE

MY TASKLIST

MY APPOINTMENTS

HEALTH NOTES

EXERCISE

NOTES TO SELF

GRATITUDE LIST

DAILY PLANNER

TODAY IS A NEW DAY FULL OF POSSIBILITY

DATE

WATER INTAKE

MY TASKLIST

MY APPOINTMENTS

HEALTH NOTES

EXERCISE

NOTES TO SELF

GRATITUDE LIST

DAILY PLANNER
TODAY IS A NEW DAY FULL OF POSSIBILITY

DATE   WATER INTAKE

MY TASKLIST   MY APPOINTMENTS

HEALTH NOTES   EXERCISE

NOTES TO SELF   GRATITUDE LIST

DAILY PLANNER
TODAY IS A NEW DAY FULL OF POSSIBILITY

DATE

WATER INTAKE

MY TASKLIST

MY APPOINTMENTS

HEALTH NOTES

EXERCISE

NOTES TO SELF

GRATITUDE LIST

DAILY PLANNER
TODAY IS A NEW DAY FULL OF POSSIBILITY

DATE

WATER INTAKE

MY TASKLIST

MY APPOINTMENTS

HEALTH NOTES

EXERCISE

NOTES TO SELF

GRATITUDE LIST

DAILY PLANNER
TODAY IS A NEW DAY FULL OF POSSIBILITY

DATE   WATER INTAKE

MY TASKLIST   MY APPOINTMENTS

HEALTH NOTES   EXERCISE

NOTES TO SELF   GRATITUDE LIST

DAILY PLANNER
TODAY IS A NEW DAY FULL OF POSSIBILITY

DATE

WATER INTAKE

MY TASKLIST

MY APPOINTMENTS

HEALTH NOTES

EXERCISE

NOTES TO SELF

GRATITUDE LIST

DAILY PLANNER

TODAY IS A NEW DAY FULL OF POSSIBILITY

DATE

WATER INTAKE

MY TASKLIST

MY APPOINTMENTS

HEALTH NOTES

EXERCISE

NOTES TO SELF

GRATITUDE LIST

DAILY PLANNER
TODAY IS A NEW DAY FULL OF POSSIBILITY

DATE

WATER INTAKE

MY TASKLIST

MY APPOINTMENTS

HEALTH NOTES

EXERCISE

NOTES TO SELF

GRATITUDE LIST

DAILY PLANNER
TODAY IS A NEW DAY FULL OF POSSIBILITY

DATE

WATER INTAKE

MY TASKLIST

MY APPOINTMENTS

HEALTH NOTES

EXERCISE

NOTES TO SELF

GRATITUDE LIST

DAILY PLANNER
TODAY IS A NEW DAY FULL OF POSSIBILITY

DATE   WATER INTAKE

MY TASKLIST   MY APPOINTMENTS

HEALTH NOTES   EXERCISE

NOTES TO SELF   GRATITUDE LIST

DAILY PLANNER
TODAY IS A NEW DAY FULL OF POSSIBILITY

DATE

WATER INTAKE

MY TASKLIST

MY APPOINTMENTS

HEALTH NOTES

EXERCISE

NOTES TO SELF

GRATITUDE LIST

DAILY PLANNER
TODAY IS A NEW DAY FULL OF POSSIBILITY

DATE

WATER INTAKE

MY TASKLIST

MY APPOINTMENTS

HEALTH NOTES

EXERCISE

NOTES TO SELF

GRATITUDE LIST

DAILY PLANNER
TODAY IS A NEW DAY FULL OF POSSIBILITY

DATE

WATER INTAKE

MY TASKLIST

MY APPOINTMENTS

HEALTH NOTES

EXERCISE

NOTES TO SELF

GRATITUDE LIST

DAILY PLANNER

TODAY IS A NEW DAY FULL OF POSSIBILITY

DATE

WATER INTAKE

MY TASKLIST

MY APPOINTMENTS

HEALTH NOTES

EXERCISE

NOTES TO SELF

GRATITUDE LIST

DAILY PLANNER
TODAY IS A NEW DAY FULL OF POSSIBILITY

DATE

WATER INTAKE

MY TASKLIST

MY APPOINTMENTS

HEALTH NOTES

EXERCISE

NOTES TO SELF

GRATITUDE LIST

DAILY PLANNER

TODAY IS A NEW DAY FULL OF POSSIBILITY

DATE

WATER INTAKE

MY TASKLIST

MY APPOINTMENTS

HEALTH NOTES

EXERCISE

NOTES TO SELF

GRATITUDE LIST

DAILY PLANNER

TODAY IS A NEW DAY FULL OF POSSIBILITY

DATE

WATER INTAKE

MY TASKLIST

MY APPOINTMENTS

HEALTH NOTES

EXERCISE

NOTES TO SELF

GRATITUDE LIST

DAILY PLANNER

TODAY IS A NEW DAY FULL OF POSSIBILITY

DATE

WATER INTAKE

MY TASKLIST

MY APPOINTMENTS

HEALTH NOTES

EXERCISE

NOTES TO SELF

GRATITUDE LIST

DAILY PLANNER

TODAY IS A NEW DAY FULL OF POSSIBILITY

DATE

WATER INTAKE

MY TASKLIST

MY APPOINTMENTS

HEALTH NOTES

EXERCISE

NOTES TO SELF

GRATITUDE LIST

DAILY PLANNER
TODAY IS A NEW DAY FULL OF POSSIBILITY

DATE

WATER INTAKE

MY TASKLIST

MY APPOINTMENTS

HEALTH NOTES

EXERCISE

NOTES TO SELF

GRATITUDE LIST

DAILY PLANNER

TODAY IS A NEW DAY FULL OF POSSIBILITY

DATE

WATER INTAKE

MY TASKLIST

MY APPOINTMENTS

HEALTH NOTES

EXERCISE

NOTES TO SELF

GRATITUDE LIST

DAILY PLANNER

TODAY IS A NEW DAY FULL OF POSSIBILITY

DATE

WATER INTAKE

MY TASKLIST

MY APPOINTMENTS

HEALTH NOTES

EXERCISE

NOTES TO SELF

GRATITUDE LIST

DAILY PLANNER

TODAY IS A NEW DAY FULL OF POSSIBILITY

DATE WATER INTAKE

MY TASKLIST MY APPOINTMENTS

HEALTH NOTES EXERCISE

NOTES TO SELF GRATITUDE LIST

DAILY PLANNER

TODAY IS A NEW DAY FULL OF POSSIBILITY

DATE

WATER INTAKE

MY TASKLIST

MY APPOINTMENTS

HEALTH NOTES

EXERCISE

NOTES TO SELF

GRATITUDE LIST

DAILY PLANNER
TODAY IS A NEW DAY FULL OF POSSIBILITY

DATE

WATER INTAKE

MY TASKLIST

MY APPOINTMENTS

HEALTH NOTES

EXERCISE

NOTES TO SELF

GRATITUDE LIST

DAILY PLANNER

TODAY IS A NEW DAY FULL OF POSSIBILITY

DATE

WATER INTAKE

MY TASKLIST

MY APPOINTMENTS

HEALTH NOTES

EXERCISE

NOTES TO SELF

GRATITUDE LIST

DAILY PLANNER
TODAY IS A NEW DAY FULL OF POSSIBILITY

DATE

WATER INTAKE

MY TASKLIST

MY APPOINTMENTS

HEALTH NOTES

EXERCISE

NOTES TO SELF

GRATITUDE LIST

DAILY PLANNER

TODAY IS A NEW DAY FULL OF POSSIBILITY

DATE

WATER INTAKE

MY TASKLIST

MY APPOINTMENTS

HEALTH NOTES

EXERCISE

NOTES TO SELF

GRATITUDE LIST

DAILY PLANNER

TODAY IS A NEW DAY FULL OF POSSIBILITY

DATE   WATER INTAKE

MY TASKLIST   MY APPOINTMENTS

HEALTH NOTES   EXERCISE

NOTES TO SELF   GRATITUDE LIST

DAILY PLANNER
TODAY IS A NEW DAY FULL OF POSSIBILITY

DATE

WATER INTAKE

MY TASKLIST

MY APPOINTMENTS

HEALTH NOTES

EXERCISE

NOTES TO SELF

GRATITUDE LIST

DAILY PLANNER
TODAY IS A NEW DAY FULL OF POSSIBILITY

DATE

WATER INTAKE

MY TASKLIST

MY APPOINTMENTS

HEALTH NOTES

EXERCISE

NOTES TO SELF

GRATITUDE LIST

DAILY PLANNER
TODAY IS A NEW DAY FULL OF POSSIBILITY

DATE   WATER INTAKE

MY TASKLIST   MY APPOINTMENTS

HEALTH NOTES   EXERCISE

NOTES TO SELF   GRATITUDE LIST

DAILY PLANNER

TODAY IS A NEW DAY FULL OF POSSIBILITY

DATE

WATER INTAKE

MY TASKLIST

MY APPOINTMENTS

HEALTH NOTES

EXERCISE

NOTES TO SELF

GRATITUDE LIST

DAILY PLANNER
TODAY IS A NEW DAY FULL OF POSSIBILITY

DATE

WATER INTAKE

MY TASKLIST

MY APPOINTMENTS

HEALTH NOTES

EXERCISE

NOTES TO SELF

GRATITUDE LIST

DAILY PLANNER

TODAY IS A NEW DAY FULL OF POSSIBILITY

DATE

WATER INTAKE

MY TASKLIST

MY APPOINTMENTS

HEALTH NOTES

EXERCISE

NOTES TO SELF

GRATITUDE LIST

DAILY PLANNER
TODAY IS A NEW DAY FULL OF POSSIBILITY

DATE

WATER INTAKE

MY TASKLIST

MY APPOINTMENTS

HEALTH NOTES

EXERCISE

NOTES TO SELF

GRATITUDE LIST

DAILY PLANNER
TODAY IS A NEW DAY FULL OF POSSIBILITY

DATE

WATER INTAKE

MY TASKLIST

MY APPOINTMENTS

HEALTH NOTES

EXERCISE

NOTES TO SELF

GRATITUDE LIST

DAILY PLANNER
TODAY IS A NEW DAY FULL OF POSSIBILITY

DATE

WATER INTAKE

MY TASKLIST

MY APPOINTMENTS

HEALTH NOTES

EXERCISE

NOTES TO SELF

GRATITUDE LIST

DAILY PLANNER

TODAY IS A NEW DAY FULL OF POSSIBILITY

DATE

WATER INTAKE

MY TASKLIST

MY APPOINTMENTS

HEALTH NOTES

EXERCISE

NOTES TO SELF

GRATITUDE LIST

DAILY PLANNER
TODAY IS A NEW DAY FULL OF POSSIBILITY

DATE

WATER INTAKE

MY TASKLIST

MY APPOINTMENTS

HEALTH NOTES

EXERCISE

NOTES TO SELF

GRATITUDE LIST

DAILY PLANNER
TODAY IS A NEW DAY FULL OF POSSIBILITY

DATE

WATER INTAKE

MY TASKLIST

MY APPOINTMENTS

HEALTH NOTES

EXERCISE

NOTES TO SELF

GRATITUDE LIST

DAILY PLANNER
TODAY IS A NEW DAY FULL OF POSSIBILITY

DATE

WATER INTAKE

MY TASKLIST

MY APPOINTMENTS

HEALTH NOTES

EXERCISE

NOTES TO SELF

GRATITUDE LIST

DAILY PLANNER

TODAY IS A NEW DAY FULL OF POSSIBILITY

DATE

WATER INTAKE

MY TASKLIST

MY APPOINTMENTS

HEALTH NOTES

EXERCISE

NOTES TO SELF

GRATITUDE LIST

DAILY PLANNER
TODAY IS A NEW DAY FULL OF POSSIBILITY

DATE

WATER INTAKE

MY TASKLIST

MY APPOINTMENTS

HEALTH NOTES

EXERCISE

NOTES TO SELF

GRATITUDE LIST

DAILY PLANNER
TODAY IS A NEW DAY FULL OF POSSIBILITY

DATE

WATER INTAKE

MY TASKLIST

MY APPOINTMENTS

HEALTH NOTES

EXERCISE

NOTES TO SELF

GRATITUDE LIST

DAILY PLANNER
TODAY IS A NEW DAY FULL OF POSSIBILITY

DATE

WATER INTAKE

MY TASKLIST

MY APPOINTMENTS

HEALTH NOTES

EXERCISE

NOTES TO SELF

GRATITUDE LIST

DAILY PLANNER

TODAY IS A NEW DAY FULL OF POSSIBILITY

DATE

WATER INTAKE

MY TASKLIST

MY APPOINTMENTS

HEALTH NOTES

EXERCISE

NOTES TO SELF

GRATITUDE LIST

DAILY PLANNER
TODAY IS A NEW DAY FULL OF POSSIBILITY

DATE

WATER INTAKE

MY TASKLIST

MY APPOINTMENTS

HEALTH NOTES

EXERCISE

NOTES TO SELF

GRATITUDE LIST

DAILY PLANNER

TODAY IS A NEW DAY FULL OF POSSIBILITY

DATE

WATER INTAKE

MY TASKLIST

MY APPOINTMENTS

HEALTH NOTES

EXERCISE

NOTES TO SELF

GRATITUDE LIST

DAILY PLANNER
TODAY IS A NEW DAY FULL OF POSSIBILITY

DATE

WATER INTAKE

MY TASKLIST

MY APPOINTMENTS

HEALTH NOTES

EXERCISE

NOTES TO SELF

GRATITUDE LIST

DAILY PLANNER
TODAY IS A NEW DAY FULL OF POSSIBILITY

DATE

WATER INTAKE

MY TASKLIST

MY APPOINTMENTS

HEALTH NOTES

EXERCISE

NOTES TO SELF

GRATITUDE LIST

DAILY PLANNER

TODAY IS A NEW DAY FULL OF POSSIBILITY

DATE

WATER INTAKE

MY TASKLIST

MY APPOINTMENTS

HEALTH NOTES

EXERCISE

NOTES TO SELF

GRATITUDE LIST

DAILY PLANNER

TODAY IS A NEW DAY FULL OF POSSIBILITY

DATE

WATER INTAKE

MY TASKLIST

MY APPOINTMENTS

HEALTH NOTES

EXERCISE

NOTES TO SELF

GRATITUDE LIST

DAILY PLANNER
TODAY IS A NEW DAY FULL OF POSSIBILITY

DATE

WATER INTAKE

MY TASKLIST

MY APPOINTMENTS

HEALTH NOTES

EXERCISE

NOTES TO SELF

GRATITUDE LIST

DAILY PLANNER
TODAY IS A NEW DAY FULL OF POSSIBILITY

DATE

WATER INTAKE

MY TASKLIST

MY APPOINTMENTS

HEALTH NOTES

EXERCISE

NOTES TO SELF

GRATITUDE LIST

DAILY PLANNER
TODAY IS A NEW DAY FULL OF POSSIBILITY

DATE

WATER INTAKE

MY TASKLIST

MY APPOINTMENTS

HEALTH NOTES

EXERCISE

NOTES TO SELF

GRATITUDE LIST

DAILY PLANNER

TODAY IS A NEW DAY FULL OF POSSIBILITY

DATE

WATER INTAKE

MY TASKLIST

MY APPOINTMENTS

HEALTH NOTES

EXERCISE

NOTES TO SELF

GRATITUDE LIST

DAILY PLANNER
TODAY IS A NEW DAY FULL OF POSSIBILITY

DATE

WATER INTAKE

MY TASKLIST

MY APPOINTMENTS

HEALTH NOTES

EXERCISE

NOTES TO SELF

GRATITUDE LIST

DAILY PLANNER
TODAY IS A NEW DAY FULL OF POSSIBILITY

DATE

WATER INTAKE

MY TASKLIST

MY APPOINTMENTS

HEALTH NOTES

EXERCISE

NOTES TO SELF

GRATITUDE LIST

DAILY PLANNER

TODAY IS A NEW DAY FULL OF POSSIBILITY

DATE

WATER INTAKE

MY TASKLIST

MY APPOINTMENTS

HEALTH NOTES

EXERCISE

NOTES TO SELF

GRATITUDE LIST

DAILY PLANNER
TODAY IS A NEW DAY FULL OF POSSIBILITY

DATE

WATER INTAKE

MY TASKLIST

MY APPOINTMENTS

HEALTH NOTES

EXERCISE

NOTES TO SELF

GRATITUDE LIST

DAILY PLANNER

TODAY IS A NEW DAY FULL OF POSSIBILITY

DATE

WATER INTAKE

MY TASKLIST

MY APPOINTMENTS

HEALTH NOTES

EXERCISE

NOTES TO SELF

GRATITUDE LIST

DAILY PLANNER
TODAY IS A NEW DAY FULL OF POSSIBILITY

DATE

WATER INTAKE

MY TASKLIST

MY APPOINTMENTS

HEALTH NOTES

EXERCISE

NOTES TO SELF

GRATITUDE LIST

DAILY PLANNER
TODAY IS A NEW DAY FULL OF POSSIBILITY

DATE

WATER INTAKE

MY TASKLIST

MY APPOINTMENTS

HEALTH NOTES

EXERCISE

NOTES TO SELF

GRATITUDE LIST

DAILY PLANNER

TODAY IS A NEW DAY FULL OF POSSIBILITY

DATE

WATER INTAKE

MY TASKLIST

MY APPOINTMENTS

HEALTH NOTES

EXERCISE

NOTES TO SELF

GRATITUDE LIST

DAILY PLANNER
TODAY IS A NEW DAY FULL OF POSSIBILITY

DATE WATER INTAKE

MY TASKLIST MY APPOINTMENTS

HEALTH NOTES EXERCISE

NOTES TO SELF GRATITUDE LIST

DAILY PLANNER

TODAY IS A NEW DAY FULL OF POSSIBILITY

DATE

WATER INTAKE

MY TASKLIST

MY APPOINTMENTS

HEALTH NOTES

EXERCISE

NOTES TO SELF

GRATITUDE LIST

DAILY PLANNER
TODAY IS A NEW DAY FULL OF POSSIBILITY

DATE

WATER INTAKE

MY TASKLIST

MY APPOINTMENTS

HEALTH NOTES

EXERCISE

NOTES TO SELF

GRATITUDE LIST

DAILY PLANNER

TODAY IS A NEW DAY FULL OF POSSIBILITY

DATE

WATER INTAKE

MY TASKLIST

MY APPOINTMENTS

HEALTH NOTES

EXERCISE

NOTES TO SELF

GRATITUDE LIST

DAILY PLANNER
TODAY IS A NEW DAY FULL OF POSSIBILITY

DATE

WATER INTAKE

MY TASKLIST

MY APPOINTMENTS

HEALTH NOTES

EXERCISE

NOTES TO SELF

GRATITUDE LIST

DAILY PLANNER
TODAY IS A NEW DAY FULL OF POSSIBILITY

DATE

WATER INTAKE

MY TASKLIST

MY APPOINTMENTS

HEALTH NOTES

EXERCISE

NOTES TO SELF

GRATITUDE LIST

DAILY PLANNER

TODAY IS A NEW DAY FULL OF POSSIBILITY

DATE

WATER INTAKE

MY TASKLIST

MY APPOINTMENTS

HEALTH NOTES

EXERCISE

NOTES TO SELF

GRATITUDE LIST

DAILY PLANNER
TODAY IS A NEW DAY FULL OF POSSIBILITY

DATE

WATER INTAKE

MY TASKLIST

MY APPOINTMENTS

HEALTH NOTES

EXERCISE

NOTES TO SELF

GRATITUDE LIST

DAILY PLANNER

TODAY IS A NEW DAY FULL OF POSSIBILITY

DATE

WATER INTAKE

MY TASKLIST

MY APPOINTMENTS

HEALTH NOTES

EXERCISE

NOTES TO SELF

GRATITUDE LIST

DAILY PLANNER
TODAY IS A NEW DAY FULL OF POSSIBILITY

DATE

WATER INTAKE

MY TASKLIST

MY APPOINTMENTS

HEALTH NOTES

EXERCISE

NOTES TO SELF

GRATITUDE LIST

DAILY PLANNER
TODAY IS A NEW DAY FULL OF POSSIBILITY

DATE

WATER INTAKE

MY TASKLIST

MY APPOINTMENTS

HEALTH NOTES

EXERCISE

NOTES TO SELF

GRATITUDE LIST

DAILY PLANNER

TODAY IS A NEW DAY FULL OF POSSIBILITY

DATE   WATER INTAKE

   MY TASKLIST   MY APPOINTMENTS

   HEALTH NOTES   EXERCISE

   NOTES TO SELF   GRATITUDE LIST

DAILY PLANNER
TODAY IS A NEW DAY FULL OF POSSIBILITY

DATE

WATER INTAKE

MY TASKLIST

MY APPOINTMENTS

HEALTH NOTES

EXERCISE

NOTES TO SELF

GRATITUDE LIST

DAILY PLANNER
TODAY IS A NEW DAY FULL OF POSSIBILITY

DATE

WATER INTAKE

MY TASKLIST

MY APPOINTMENTS

HEALTH NOTES

EXERCISE

NOTES TO SELF

GRATITUDE LIST

DAILY PLANNER
TODAY IS A NEW DAY FULL OF POSSIBILITY

DATE

WATER INTAKE

MY TASKLIST

MY APPOINTMENTS

HEALTH NOTES

EXERCISE

NOTES TO SELF

GRATITUDE LIST

DAILY PLANNER
TODAY IS A NEW DAY FULL OF POSSIBILITY

DATE

WATER INTAKE

MY TASKLIST

MY APPOINTMENTS

HEALTH NOTES

EXERCISE

NOTES TO SELF

GRATITUDE LIST

DAILY PLANNER

TODAY IS A NEW DAY FULL OF POSSIBILITY

DATE

WATER INTAKE

MY TASKLIST

MY APPOINTMENTS

HEALTH NOTES

EXERCISE

NOTES TO SELF

GRATITUDE LIST

DAILY PLANNER

TODAY IS A NEW DAY FULL OF POSSIBILITY

DATE

WATER INTAKE

MY TASKLIST

MY APPOINTMENTS

HEALTH NOTES

EXERCISE

NOTES TO SELF

GRATITUDE LIST

DAILY PLANNER
TODAY IS A NEW DAY FULL OF POSSIBILITY

DATE

WATER INTAKE

MY TASKLIST

MY APPOINTMENTS

HEALTH NOTES

EXERCISE

NOTES TO SELF

GRATITUDE LIST

DAILY PLANNER

TODAY IS A NEW DAY FULL OF POSSIBILITY

DATE

WATER INTAKE

MY TASKLIST

MY APPOINTMENTS

HEALTH NOTES

EXERCISE

NOTES TO SELF

GRATITUDE LIST

DAILY PLANNER

TODAY IS A NEW DAY FULL OF POSSIBILITY

DATE

WATER INTAKE

MY TASKLIST

MY APPOINTMENTS

HEALTH NOTES

EXERCISE

NOTES TO SELF

GRATITUDE LIST

DAILY PLANNER
TODAY IS A NEW DAY FULL OF POSSIBILITY

DATE

WATER INTAKE

MY TASKLIST

MY APPOINTMENTS

HEALTH NOTES

EXERCISE

NOTES TO SELF

GRATITUDE LIST

DAILY PLANNER
TODAY IS A NEW DAY FULL OF POSSIBILITY

DATE

WATER INTAKE

MY TASKLIST

MY APPOINTMENTS

HEALTH NOTES

EXERCISE

NOTES TO SELF

GRATITUDE LIST

DAILY PLANNER

TODAY IS A NEW DAY FULL OF POSSIBILITY

DATE WATER INTAKE

MY TASKLIST MY APPOINTMENTS

HEALTH NOTES EXERCISE

NOTES TO SELF GRATITUDE LIST

DAILY PLANNER
TODAY IS A NEW DAY FULL OF POSSIBILITY

DATE

WATER INTAKE

MY TASKLIST

MY APPOINTMENTS

HEALTH NOTES

EXERCISE

NOTES TO SELF

GRATITUDE LIST

DAILY PLANNER

TODAY IS A NEW DAY FULL OF POSSIBILITY

DATE

WATER INTAKE

MY TASKLIST

MY APPOINTMENTS

HEALTH NOTES

EXERCISE

NOTES TO SELF

GRATITUDE LIST

DAILY PLANNER

TODAY IS A NEW DAY FULL OF POSSIBILITY

DATE

WATER INTAKE

MY TASKLIST

MY APPOINTMENTS

HEALTH NOTES

EXERCISE

NOTES TO SELF

GRATITUDE LIST

DAILY PLANNER
TODAY IS A NEW DAY FULL OF POSSIBILITY

DATE

WATER INTAKE

MY TASKLIST

MY APPOINTMENTS

HEALTH NOTES

EXERCISE

NOTES TO SELF

GRATITUDE LIST

DAILY PLANNER

TODAY IS A NEW DAY FULL OF POSSIBILITY

DATE

WATER INTAKE

MY TASKLIST

MY APPOINTMENTS

HEALTH NOTES

EXERCISE

NOTES TO SELF

GRATITUDE LIST

DAILY PLANNER

TODAY IS A NEW DAY FULL OF POSSIBILITY

DATE

WATER INTAKE

MY TASKLIST

MY APPOINTMENTS

HEALTH NOTES

EXERCISE

NOTES TO SELF

GRATITUDE LIST

DAILY PLANNER
TODAY IS A NEW DAY FULL OF POSSIBILITY

DATE

WATER INTAKE

MY TASKLIST

MY APPOINTMENTS

HEALTH NOTES

EXERCISE

NOTES TO SELF

GRATITUDE LIST

DAILY PLANNER

TODAY IS A NEW DAY FULL OF POSSIBILITY

DATE WATER INTAKE

MY TASKLIST MY APPOINTMENTS

HEALTH NOTES EXERCISE

NOTES TO SELF GRATITUDE LIST

DAILY PLANNER

TODAY IS A NEW DAY FULL OF POSSIBILITY

DATE

WATER INTAKE

MY TASKLIST

MY APPOINTMENTS

HEALTH NOTES

EXERCISE

NOTES TO SELF

GRATITUDE LIST

DAILY PLANNER
TODAY IS A NEW DAY FULL OF POSSIBILITY

DATE

WATER INTAKE

MY TASKLIST

MY APPOINTMENTS

HEALTH NOTES

EXERCISE

NOTES TO SELF

GRATITUDE LIST

DAILY PLANNER
TODAY IS A NEW DAY FULL OF POSSIBILITY

DATE

WATER INTAKE

MY TASKLIST

MY APPOINTMENTS

HEALTH NOTES

EXERCISE

NOTES TO SELF

GRATITUDE LIST

DAILY PLANNER
TODAY IS A NEW DAY FULL OF POSSIBILITY

DATE

WATER INTAKE

MY TASKLIST

MY APPOINTMENTS

HEALTH NOTES

EXERCISE

NOTES TO SELF

GRATITUDE LIST

DAILY PLANNER
TODAY IS A NEW DAY FULL OF POSSIBILITY

DATE　　　　　　WATER INTAKE

MY TASKLIST　　　　　　MY APPOINTMENTS

HEALTH NOTES　　　　　　EXERCISE

NOTES TO SELF　　　　　　GRATITUDE LIST

DAILY PLANNER

TODAY IS A NEW DAY FULL OF POSSIBILITY

DATE

WATER INTAKE

MY TASKLIST

MY APPOINTMENTS

HEALTH NOTES

EXERCISE

NOTES TO SELF

GRATITUDE LIST

DAILY PLANNER
TODAY IS A NEW DAY FULL OF POSSIBILITY

DATE

WATER INTAKE

MY TASKLIST

MY APPOINTMENTS

HEALTH NOTES

EXERCISE

NOTES TO SELF

GRATITUDE LIST

DAILY PLANNER

TODAY IS A NEW DAY FULL OF POSSIBILITY

DATE

WATER INTAKE

MY TASKLIST

MY APPOINTMENTS

HEALTH NOTES

EXERCISE

NOTES TO SELF

GRATITUDE LIST

DAILY PLANNER

TODAY IS A NEW DAY FULL OF POSSIBILITY

DATE

WATER INTAKE

MY TASKLIST

MY APPOINTMENTS

HEALTH NOTES

EXERCISE

NOTES TO SELF

GRATITUDE LIST

DAILY PLANNER

TODAY IS A NEW DAY FULL OF POSSIBILITY

DATE

WATER INTAKE

MY TASKLIST

MY APPOINTMENTS

HEALTH NOTES

EXERCISE

NOTES TO SELF

GRATITUDE LIST

DAILY PLANNER
TODAY IS A NEW DAY FULL OF POSSIBILITY

DATE WATER INTAKE

MY TASKLIST MY APPOINTMENTS

HEALTH NOTES EXERCISE

NOTES TO SELF GRATITUDE LIST

DAILY PLANNER

TODAY IS A NEW DAY FULL OF POSSIBILITY

DATE

WATER INTAKE

MY TASKLIST

MY APPOINTMENTS

HEALTH NOTES

EXERCISE

NOTES TO SELF

GRATITUDE LIST

DAILY PLANNER
TODAY IS A NEW DAY FULL OF POSSIBILITY

DATE

WATER INTAKE

MY TASKLIST

MY APPOINTMENTS

HEALTH NOTES

EXERCISE

NOTES TO SELF

GRATITUDE LIST

DAILY PLANNER

TODAY IS A NEW DAY FULL OF POSSIBILITY

DATE

WATER INTAKE

MY TASKLIST

MY APPOINTMENTS

HEALTH NOTES

EXERCISE

NOTES TO SELF

GRATITUDE LIST

DAILY PLANNER

TODAY IS A NEW DAY FULL OF POSSIBILITY

DATE

WATER INTAKE

MY TASKLIST

MY APPOINTMENTS

HEALTH NOTES

EXERCISE

NOTES TO SELF

GRATITUDE LIST

DAILY PLANNER

TODAY IS A NEW DAY FULL OF POSSIBILITY

DATE

WATER INTAKE

MY TASKLIST

MY APPOINTMENTS

HEALTH NOTES

EXERCISE

NOTES TO SELF

GRATITUDE LIST

DAILY PLANNER

TODAY IS A NEW DAY FULL OF POSSIBILITY

DATE

WATER INTAKE

MY TASKLIST

MY APPOINTMENTS

HEALTH NOTES

EXERCISE

NOTES TO SELF

GRATITUDE LIST

DAILY PLANNER

TODAY IS A NEW DAY FULL OF POSSIBILITY

DATE

WATER INTAKE

MY TASKLIST

MY APPOINTMENTS

HEALTH NOTES

EXERCISE

NOTES TO SELF

GRATITUDE LIST

DAILY PLANNER

TODAY IS A NEW DAY FULL OF POSSIBILITY

DATE

WATER INTAKE

MY TASKLIST

MY APPOINTMENTS

HEALTH NOTES

EXERCISE

NOTES TO SELF

GRATITUDE LIST

DAILY PLANNER

TODAY IS A NEW DAY FULL OF POSSIBILITY

DATE

WATER INTAKE

MY TASKLIST

MY APPOINTMENTS

HEALTH NOTES

EXERCISE

NOTES TO SELF

GRATITUDE LIST

DAILY PLANNER

TODAY IS A NEW DAY FULL OF POSSIBILITY

DATE

WATER INTAKE

MY TASKLIST

MY APPOINTMENTS

HEALTH NOTES

EXERCISE

NOTES TO SELF

GRATITUDE LIST

DAILY PLANNER

TODAY IS A NEW DAY FULL OF POSSIBILITY

DATE

WATER INTAKE

MY TASKLIST

MY APPOINTMENTS

HEALTH NOTES

EXERCISE

NOTES TO SELF

GRATITUDE LIST

DAILY PLANNER

TODAY IS A NEW DAY FULL OF POSSIBILITY

DATE   WATER INTAKE

MY TASKLIST   MY APPOINTMENTS

HEALTH NOTES   EXERCISE

NOTES TO SELF   GRATITUDE LIST

DAILY PLANNER

TODAY IS A NEW DAY FULL OF POSSIBILITY

DATE

WATER INTAKE

MY TASKLIST

MY APPOINTMENTS

HEALTH NOTES

EXERCISE

NOTES TO SELF

GRATITUDE LIST

DAILY PLANNER

TODAY IS A NEW DAY FULL OF POSSIBILITY

DATE

WATER INTAKE

MY TASKLIST

MY APPOINTMENTS

HEALTH NOTES

EXERCISE

NOTES TO SELF

GRATITUDE LIST

DAILY PLANNER
TODAY IS A NEW DAY FULL OF POSSIBILITY

DATE

WATER INTAKE

MY TASKLIST

MY APPOINTMENTS

HEALTH NOTES

EXERCISE

NOTES TO SELF

GRATITUDE LIST

DAILY PLANNER
TODAY IS A NEW DAY FULL OF POSSIBILITY

DATE

WATER INTAKE

MY TASKLIST

MY APPOINTMENTS

HEALTH NOTES

EXERCISE

NOTES TO SELF

GRATITUDE LIST

DAILY PLANNER

TODAY IS A NEW DAY FULL OF POSSIBILITY

DATE

WATER INTAKE

MY TASKLIST

MY APPOINTMENTS

HEALTH NOTES

EXERCISE

NOTES TO SELF

GRATITUDE LIST

DAILY PLANNER
TODAY IS A NEW DAY FULL OF POSSIBILITY

DATE

WATER INTAKE

MY TASKLIST

MY APPOINTMENTS

HEALTH NOTES

EXERCISE

NOTES TO SELF

GRATITUDE LIST

DAILY PLANNER
TODAY IS A NEW DAY FULL OF POSSIBILITY

DATE

WATER INTAKE

MY TASKLIST

MY APPOINTMENTS

HEALTH NOTES

EXERCISE

NOTES TO SELF

GRATITUDE LIST

DAILY PLANNER
TODAY IS A NEW DAY FULL OF POSSIBILITY

DATE

WATER INTAKE

MY TASKLIST

MY APPOINTMENTS

HEALTH NOTES

EXERCISE

NOTES TO SELF

GRATITUDE LIST

DAILY PLANNER
TODAY IS A NEW DAY FULL OF POSSIBILITY

DATE

WATER INTAKE

MY TASKLIST

MY APPOINTMENTS

HEALTH NOTES

EXERCISE

NOTES TO SELF

GRATITUDE LIST

DAILY PLANNER
TODAY IS A NEW DAY FULL OF POSSIBILITY

DATE

WATER INTAKE

MY TASKLIST

MY APPOINTMENTS

HEALTH NOTES

EXERCISE

NOTES TO SELF

GRATITUDE LIST

DAILY PLANNER

TODAY IS A NEW DAY FULL OF POSSIBILITY

DATE

WATER INTAKE

MY TASKLIST

MY APPOINTMENTS

HEALTH NOTES

EXERCISE

NOTES TO SELF

GRATITUDE LIST

DAILY PLANNER
TODAY IS A NEW DAY FULL OF POSSIBILITY

DATE　　　　　　　WATER INTAKE

MY TASKLIST　　　　　　　MY APPOINTMENTS

HEALTH NOTES　　　　　　　EXERCISE

NOTES TO SELF　　　　　　　GRATITUDE LIST

DAILY PLANNER

TODAY IS A NEW DAY FULL OF POSSIBILITY

DATE

WATER INTAKE

MY TASKLIST

MY APPOINTMENTS

HEALTH NOTES

EXERCISE

NOTES TO SELF

GRATITUDE LIST

DAILY PLANNER

TODAY IS A NEW DAY FULL OF POSSIBILITY

DATE

WATER INTAKE

MY TASKLIST

MY APPOINTMENTS

HEALTH NOTES

EXERCISE

NOTES TO SELF

GRATITUDE LIST

DAILY PLANNER
TODAY IS A NEW DAY FULL OF POSSIBILITY

DATE WATER INTAKE

MY TASKLIST MY APPOINTMENTS

HEALTH NOTES EXERCISE

NOTES TO SELF GRATITUDE LIST

DAILY PLANNER
TODAY IS A NEW DAY FULL OF POSSIBILITY

DATE

WATER INTAKE

MY TASKLIST

MY APPOINTMENTS

HEALTH NOTES

EXERCISE

NOTES TO SELF

GRATITUDE LIST

DAILY PLANNER

TODAY IS A NEW DAY FULL OF POSSIBILITY

DATE

WATER INTAKE

MY TASKLIST

MY APPOINTMENTS

HEALTH NOTES

EXERCISE

NOTES TO SELF

GRATITUDE LIST

DAILY PLANNER

TODAY IS A NEW DAY FULL OF POSSIBILITY

DATE

WATER INTAKE

MY TASKLIST

MY APPOINTMENTS

HEALTH NOTES

EXERCISE

NOTES TO SELF

GRATITUDE LIST

DAILY PLANNER

TODAY IS A NEW DAY FULL OF POSSIBILITY

DATE

WATER INTAKE

MY TASKLIST

MY APPOINTMENTS

HEALTH NOTES

EXERCISE

NOTES TO SELF

GRATITUDE LIST

DAILY PLANNER
TODAY IS A NEW DAY FULL OF POSSIBILITY

DATE

WATER INTAKE

MY TASKLIST

MY APPOINTMENTS

HEALTH NOTES

EXERCISE

NOTES TO SELF

GRATITUDE LIST

DAILY PLANNER

TODAY IS A NEW DAY FULL OF POSSIBILITY

DATE

WATER INTAKE

MY TASKLIST

MY APPOINTMENTS

HEALTH NOTES

EXERCISE

NOTES TO SELF

GRATITUDE LIST

DAILY PLANNER
TODAY IS A NEW DAY FULL OF POSSIBILITY

DATE

WATER INTAKE

MY TASKLIST

MY APPOINTMENTS

HEALTH NOTES

EXERCISE

NOTES TO SELF

GRATITUDE LIST

DAILY PLANNER

TODAY IS A NEW DAY FULL OF POSSIBILITY

DATE

WATER INTAKE

MY TASKLIST

MY APPOINTMENTS

HEALTH NOTES

EXERCISE

NOTES TO SELF

GRATITUDE LIST

DAILY PLANNER

TODAY IS A NEW DAY FULL OF POSSIBILITY

DATE

WATER INTAKE

MY TASKLIST

MY APPOINTMENTS

HEALTH NOTES

EXERCISE

NOTES TO SELF

GRATITUDE LIST

DAILY PLANNER
TODAY IS A NEW DAY FULL OF POSSIBILITY

DATE

WATER INTAKE

MY TASKLIST

MY APPOINTMENTS

HEALTH NOTES

EXERCISE

NOTES TO SELF

GRATITUDE LIST

DAILY PLANNER

TODAY IS A NEW DAY FULL OF POSSIBILITY

DATE

WATER INTAKE

MY TASKLIST

MY APPOINTMENTS

HEALTH NOTES

EXERCISE

NOTES TO SELF

GRATITUDE LIST

DAILY PLANNER

TODAY IS A NEW DAY FULL OF POSSIBILITY

DATE

WATER INTAKE

MY TASKLIST

MY APPOINTMENTS

HEALTH NOTES

EXERCISE

NOTES TO SELF

GRATITUDE LIST

www.ingramcontent.com/pod-product-compliance
Lightning Source LLC
Chambersburg PA
CBHW062049290426
44109CB00027B/2771